Let Freedom Ring

John Charles Frémont
Western Pathfinder

W0006497

by Barbara Witteman

Consultant
Robert Moore, Historian
Jefferson National Expansion Memorial
St. Louis, Missouri

Bridgestone Books
an imprint of Capstone Press
Mankato, Minnesota

Bridgestone Books are published by Capstone Press
151 Good Counsel Drive, P.O. Box 669, Mankato, Minnesota 56002
http://www.capstone-press.com

Printed in the United States of America

Library of Congress Cataloging-in-Publication Data
Witteman, Barbara.
      John Charles Frémont: Western Pathfinder/by Barbara Witteman.
              p. cm. — (Let freedom ring)
      Summary: A biography of the nineteenth-century soldier, politician, and explorer whose many expeditions helped open up the western territories to settlers.
      ISBN 0-7368-1348-9 (hardcover)
      1. Frémont, John Charles, 1813–1890—Juvenile literature. 2. Explorers—United States—Biography—Juvenile literature. 3. Explorers—West (U.S.)—Biography—Juvenile literature. 4. West (U.S.)—Discovery and exploration—Juvenile literature. 5. Generals—United States—Biography—Juvenile literature. 6. Presidential candidates—United States—Biography—Juvenile literature. [1. Frémont, John Charles, 1813–1890. 2. Explorers. 3. West (U.S.)—Discovery and exploration.]
      I. Title. II. Series.
      E415.9.F8 W58 2003
      979'.02'092—dc21   2001007880

Editorial Credits
Charles Pederson, editor; Kia Adams, series designer; Erin Scott, SARIN Creative, illustrator; Jennifer Schonborn and Juliette Peters, book designers; Kelly Garvin, photo researcher; Karen Risch, product planning editor

Photo Credits
Stock Montage, Inc., cover (large), 25, 40; Stockbyte, cover (small), 4, 12, 20, 28, 34; Corbis, 5, 23; Minnesota Historical Society/Phil Hutchins, 6–7; PhotoSphere Images, 7, 11 (right), 15 (right), 27 (right), 31 (right), 37 (right), 43 (bottom); Bettmann/Corbis, 9, 33; North Wind Picture Archives, 11 (left), 21, 29, 31 (left), 43 (top); Hulton/Archive, 13, 15 (left), 27 (left), 35, 37 (left), 38, 42; courtesy of Bob Graham, 16; the Society of California Pioneers, 24

To Ryan. May you continue to explore life to its fullest.

1 2 3 4 5 6 07 06 05 04 03 02

Table of Contents

Chapter One

Early Experiences

On January 21, 1813, John Charles Frémont was born in Savannah, Georgia. His parents were Jean Charles Frémon and Anne Whiting Pryor. Jean was from France and taught French in America. Anne was already married when she met and fell in love with Jean. Anne left her husband and ran away with Jean to Savannah, Georgia.

Jean died in 1818, and Anne decided to move her three children to Charleston, South Carolina. She ran a boardinghouse there. This establishment was like a hotel where people stayed for long periods of time. Anne added the letter *t* to the name Frémon to make her children seem more American.

At age 14, John got a job as a law clerk. His employer offered to pay for John's college education. But John decided he liked being outside more than being in classrooms. He skipped many classes, which lowered his grades. In 1831, the college told him to leave because of poor grades.

As an adult, John Charles Frémont was a soldier.
He was born in Savannah, Georgia.

John next got a job as a math teacher aboard a navy ship. Teaching brought him back to books. He found a Dutch book on astronomy, or the study of space. He could not understand the Dutch words, but he loved the book's maps of star patterns. He studied the math examples that showed how to find a location on the earth's surface.

Surveying Unexplored Areas

In 1835, John's teaching job ended. He then helped survey a train route from Charleston to Cincinnati, Ohio. Surveyors measure the land so they can make a map of it. When this job ended, John was hired to help survey land that the Cherokee Indian nation claimed. John loved to work as a surveyor. In 1837, he entered the U.S. Army engineering school to receive further training.

Joseph Nicollet was a famous explorer, talented scientist, and scholar. In 1838, he was going to survey the land between the Mississippi and Missouri Rivers.

He hired John to help with the project. John's first job was ordering supplies.

Nicollet and his men met in the busy city of St. Louis, Missouri. St. Louis is located near the place where the Missouri River flows into the Mississippi River.

In May 1838, Nicollet's surveying trip began. His men took a steamboat from St. Louis to Fort Snelling, located in present-day Minnesota. From there, they headed west. The men marked river courses on maps they made. They met different

In 1838, Fort Snelling was an important U.S. military and trading post. Nicollet's surveyors left Fort Snelling to survey areas to the west.

American Indian peoples. They kept careful records of their trip. Before winter came, the group returned to St. Louis. Nicollet and John went to Washington, D.C., to deliver the group's report to the U.S. government.

The following spring, Nicollet and his men continued their survey. The group explored much of what is now eastern North Dakota. They explored the Red River of the North, the James and Sheyenne Rivers, and Devil's Lake.

In 1839, Nicollet and John wrote their final report in Washington, D.C. There, John met Thomas Hart Benton. Benton was a U.S. senator from Missouri. He wanted the land west of the Mississippi River to be explored. He invited John to eat dinner at his home on many evenings to discuss these plans. The two men became friends.

Falling in Love

John soon met Benton's daughter, Jessie. The two fell in love. Jessie's parents did not think an army man was a good match for their daughter. They also disliked the difference in John's and Jessie's ages. John was 11 years older than Jessie.

Meeting the Dakota

The Nicollet expedition met people of the Dakota nation and invited them to a meal. John described what he saw.

"When all was ready the feast began. With the first mouthful each Indian silently laid down his spoon, and each looked at the other . . . Mr. Nicollet had put among our [food] some Swiss cheese, and to give flavor to the soup a liberal portion of this had been put into the kettles. Until this strange flavor was accounted for the Indians thought they were being poisoned; but, the cheese being shown to them and explanations made, confidence was restored; and . . . the dinner party went on . . ." The painting below shows some Dakota people about the time of the Nicollet expedition.

Courtship of John and Jessie

John and Jessie met when he brought her older sister to a school concert. Jessie was not yet 16 years old, but two men had already asked to marry her. Her parents liked John but did not want him as a son-in-law because he was poor and he was in the army. They did not think John had a bright future. Jessie's mother was so upset that she and her husband arranged for John to be sent on a surveying trip. She thought his absence would stop the feelings Jessie had for John. When John returned, their feelings were as strong as ever.

Benton and his wife arranged for John to be sent away on a job. On June 4, 1841, John left to survey the Des Moines River in Iowa Territory. Jessie's parents hoped John would forget her on this trip to make sketches, maps, and notes.

In mid-August, John returned to Washington, D.C. He had not forgotten Jessie during the trip. John and Jessie met often and soon decided to get married. Jessie and John were not of the Roman Catholic faith. But a Catholic priest was the only person willing to marry them without the knowledge of Jessie's parents. John and Jessie married secretly on October 19, 1841.

Jessie's parents were angry when they learned of the marriage. Jessie convinced her parents how much she loved John. They finally accepted the marriage, and John moved into the Bentons' home.

Jessie Benton married John in 1841. She was a talented writer and helped him write several books.

Chapter Two

The First Two Expeditions

Thomas Hart Benton believed God wanted the people of the United States to take over the entire continent even if someone already claimed it. Benton wanted government and public support of this belief, called Manifest Destiny.

In 1804, Meriwether Lewis and William Clark explored the area along the Missouri River. Benton wanted more information about the land west of the Mississippi River than the Lewis and Clark Expedition provided. John seemed the perfect leader for a long trip of exploration, called an expedition.

In June 1842, the expedition left St. Louis without hiring a guide. As the group traveled up the Missouri River by paddleboat, John talked with a man named Kit Carson. Carson was headed west to his mountain home. John discovered that Carson was familiar with much of the West. He hired Carson to guide the expedition.

Thomas Hart Benton strongly believed in Manifest Destiny. As a U.S. senator, Benton was an important supporter of John's expeditions. This illustration shows Benton in about 1845.

South Pass

South Pass is near present-day South Pass City, Wyoming. The pass is a gentle rise at the Continental Divide. Here, rivers to the west flow toward the Pacific Ocean. Rivers to the east flow toward the Mississippi River and the Gulf of Mexico. South Pass is 20 miles (32 kilometers) wide and 7,550 feet (2,300 meters) above sea level. During the early and mid-1800s, about 500,000 settlers crossed South Pass. The last recorded covered wagon crossed it in 1912. Wagon tracks are still visible at South Pass.

On July 15, the group reached Fort Laramie, in present-day Wyoming. Carson led the group to South Pass. This pass was the easiest place to cross the Rocky Mountains. John and some of his men climbed a mountain in the Wind River Mountains that they named Frémont Peak. The men needed 42 days to cross South Pass and return to Fort Laramie. On October 17, the group was back in St. Louis.

John reached Washington, D.C., 12 days later. On November 13, 1842, John and Jessie's first child, Elizabeth, was born there.

The Report on the First Expedition

In Washington, D.C., John gathered his expedition notes but had trouble writing his report. The pressure of trying to write gave him headaches and nosebleeds. He talked to Jessie about the trouble he was having. She suggested that John read his notes aloud to her. She would then write the report. John found it easier to tell his story than to write it. Jessie helped make the report interesting to read.

In March 1843, John's report was published. Its title was *A Report on an Exploration of the*

This drawing shows John heroically placing an American flag on Frémont Peak in 1842.

Country Lying between the Missouri River and the Rocky Mountains on the Line of the Kansas and Great Platte Rivers. Many people read the report and became eager to settle the areas that John described.

The Second Expedition

John's second expedition left St. Louis in May 1843. His orders were to cross South Pass again and continue on to the Columbia River. He planned to find the source, or start, of many rivers, including those flowing toward California. He planned to return along the Oregon Trail.

The members of John's expedition struggle through winter snows in the Sierra Nevada Mountains.

Jessie's Writings

As a young woman, Jessie Frémont edited her father's speeches. When her husband, John, read his notes to her, she had to sit perfectly still for hours. Even the smallest movement would upset John and break his concentration. Jessie made John's reports more lively. Jessie wrote for magazines like *Harper's*, *Wide Awake,* and *Will and Way.* She also wrote a book about John's Civil War experiences called *Story of the Guard.*

What John had in mind is not clear, but he did not completely follow his orders. In October, he reached the Columbia River. Instead of returning east, he turned south into the Sierra Nevada. The group headed toward California.

The group spent a difficult winter in the Sierra Nevada. They were lost and hungry much of the time. On March 8, 1844, they reached Sutter's Fort in northern California. John Sutter told John that California was a promising land. Seeing Sutter's green fields and busy workshops, John believed this was true.

After John's men rested, they headed home on March 22. The group followed a trail across the Mojave Desert toward the Great Salt Lake. Trappers had been through this area, but there were no written records of what they had seen. John took many notes. From the lake, the group went east across the Rocky Mountains. After 14 months away from St. Louis, John reached the city again on August 6, 1844.

The Report on the Second Expedition

John again read his expedition notes aloud to Jessie. She wrote the final report in an interesting and easy-to-read way. The report described the Oregon Trail. John and Jessie wrote of the beauty of the land. They also told of dry water holes and swarms of mosquitoes. They told of days that were freezing cold in the morning and boiling hot in the afternoon.

In February 1845, John and Jessie finished their report. The U.S. Congress ordered 10,000 copies to be printed. Because of John's discoveries, many people considered his expedition the greatest since Lewis and Clark's expedition. John received a higher rank in the army and became a national hero.

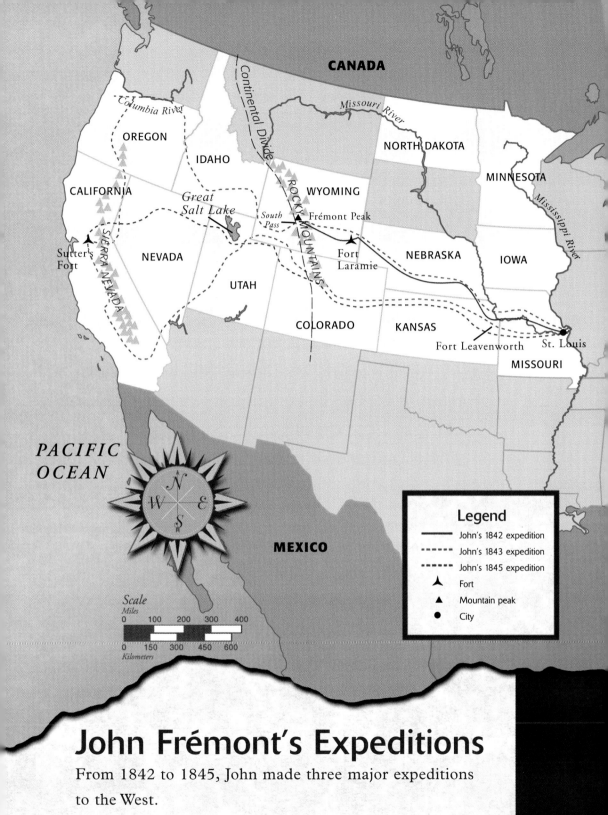

CANADA

Continental Divide

Columbia River

Missouri River

OREGON

IDAHO

NORTH DAKOTA

MINNESOTA

Mississippi River

CALIFORNIA

Great Salt Lake

ROCKY MOUNTAINS

WYOMING

Frémont Peak

South Pass

SIERRA NEVADA

Sutter's Fort

NEVADA

Fort Laramie

NEBRASKA

IOWA

UTAH

COLORADO

KANSAS

Fort Leavenworth

St. Louis

MISSOURI

PACIFIC OCEAN

N W E S

MEXICO

Legend
——	John's 1842 expedition
- - -	John's 1843 expedition
– – –	John's 1845 expedition
⌃	Fort
▲	Mountain peak
●	City

Scale
Miles
0   100   200   300   400

0   150   300   450   600
Kilometers

John Frémont's Expeditions

From 1842 to 1845, John made three major expeditions to the West.

Chapter Three

The Third Expedition

In May 1845, John received orders for a third expedition. He would survey the area near Bent's Fort in southern Colorado. The fort was a major trading post for trappers and American Indians.

John's orders were to explore the rivers that make up the border between present-day Oklahoma and Texas. The expedition left St. Louis in the spring of 1845 and arrived at Bent's Fort on August 3. John again asked Kit Carson to guide the expedition. He planned to be finished by the end of December.

John again disobeyed his orders. He did not return to St. Louis in December. Instead, he crossed the Great Basin in modern-day Utah and Nevada. He arrived at Sutter's Fort in early December. John later explained that the U.S. government gave him secret orders to learn more about California, but no one knows for sure.

John (carrying sword) sometimes wore a uniform like this
when he was on an expedition.

In 1845, Mexico owned California. John left his men at Sutter's Fort and visited Monterey and Yerba Buena, later called San Francisco. These were the main settlements in northern California.

The Mexican authorities questioned John. He told them he was an engineer, not a military officer. He said that the 60 soldiers with him were not soldiers but peaceful civilians. The Mexicans were suspicious but allowed the men to stay in the Santa Clara Valley.

War with Mexico

In March 1846, the Mexican government decided that Frémont and his men should leave California. John refused. He built a log fort on a hill that overlooked the Mexican army in the Santa Clara Valley. The Mexicans prepared to fight him. But John decided to leave for Oregon rather than fight.

A messenger found John and told him that the United States had declared war on Mexico. John told his men that they were a military unit instead of an exploring group. They returned to California.

At Sutter's Fort, more than 230 men called "Los Osos" joined John's unit. Los Osos is a Spanish

The Great Basin

The Great Basin covers about 190,000 square miles (492,000 square kilometers) of land. Its borders are the Mojave Desert on the south, the Columbia Plateau on the north, the Sierra Nevada on the west, and the Wasatch Mountains on the east.

Past explorers called the area a desert. This description caused people to avoid the area for many years. But John surveyed the eastern part of the Great Basin in 1845 and wrote positive things about it.

John's report strongly influenced a religious group called the Church of Jesus Christ of Latter-day Saints. Members of this religion eventually settled near the Great Salt Lake in present-day Utah to practice their religion in peace. The drawing below illustrates Salt Lake City about 1850.

The Bear Flag

A nephew of Mary Todd Lincoln, Abraham Lincoln's wife, received credit for designing the California Bear Flag. William L. Todd put a red star in the upper corner of a piece of brown cloth that was 54 inches (137 centimeters) long. He may have painted the star or colored it with berry juice. A grizzly bear faced the star. The middle of the flag carried the words *California Republic*. Los Osos used the flag during their fight in California.

phrase meaning "the bears." John and Los Osos marched to the town of Sonoma, which other Americans had captured. Los Osos asked John to lead them.

U.S. warships and army troops arrived to fight in California. In January 1847, the Mexicans surrendered. The war in California had lasted only a few months. The rest of the Mexican War lasted until early 1848.

Governor and Prisoner

On January 16, U.S. Navy commander Robert Stockton named John governor of California. That same day, U.S. Army General Stephen Kearny ordered John to take no military action by himself. Kearny commanded the Army of the West.

In 1846, John (holding flag) led a group of California settlers who declared themselves independent of Mexico.

John was caught between the two commanders. Stockton had no authority to name John governor, but John enjoyed his new power. Kearny ordered John to meet him in Monterey, but John did not want to obey Kearny's order. He delayed meeting Kearny until March.

Court-Martial

Kearny was angry with John's actions in California and ordered John to return with him to Washington, D.C. On August 22, 1847, Kearny's group reached Fort Leavenworth, Kansas. Kearny arrested John for acting against proper authority, disobeying orders, and acting in an unmilitary way.

John was in the army, so he had a military trial called a court-martial. It started on November 2 in Washington, D.C. On January 31, 1848, John was found guilty of all three charges.

President James Polk offered John a pardon, but John refused to take it. He believed that accepting it would be like admitting he was guilty. Instead, he left the army.

John returned to his family. Jessie again helped him write a report on his activities. The report was titled *Geographical Memoir upon Upper California, in Illustration of His Map of Oregon and California.* Thousands of people read this report.

U.S. Army General Stephen Kearny arrested John in Kansas. He accused John of disobeying orders and several other crimes. This illustration shows Kearny about 1850.

Chapter Four

The Deadly Fourth Expedition

John's father-in-law, Thomas Hart Benton, wanted a railroad to be built across the United States. He thought a route that ran from New York to St. Louis to San Francisco would work best. Other groups were already exploring possible train routes. Benton wanted John to explore and survey the St. Louis to San Francisco route.

Congress would not pay for John's expedition, so Benton went to businessmen from St. Louis. He explained that a rail line through St. Louis would be good for their businesses. The businessmen agreed to buy supplies for John's expedition but not to pay for wages. The 34 men of the expedition received no pay for their work and had to provide their own horses.

In early October 1848, the men left St. Louis. When they reached Bent's Fort, deep snow already covered the Rocky Mountains. John insisted on continuing the trip, even

Surveyors for the transcontinental railroad often had to cross difficult country to do their job. Thomas Hart Benton wanted John to find a good rail route through the Rocky Mountains.

though people at the fort said he should wait until spring. John bragged that his group could cross the snowy mountains in 35 days. Kit Carson was not available, and Old Bill Williams was the only other guide willing to lead the group. The expedition left the safety of Bent's Fort in November.

Crossing the Mountains

John soon saw that a railroad could not be built where Benton wanted it. Knowing this, John might have turned south toward warmer weather. Instead, John and Williams discussed other possible routes to follow. John decided to continue the trip through the mountains. The group began to struggle in the freezing temperatures and deep snow. John blamed Williams for the decision. Williams blamed John.

In the mountains, the men faced 50-foot (15-meter) snowdrifts. Blizzards were a constant threat. John became sick, and many of the men were frostbitten. The glare of the snow blinded some of them. They had poor shelter and little food. Their animals began to die. As the animals died, the men ate them. Finally, the group could go no farther.

John sent four men 160 miles (257 kilometers) to Taos, New Mexico. Kit Carson lived there. John believed his friend would help the expedition. When the four men did not return, John and others left to find them.

Six days later, John's group reached the first group. One man in that group had died. The others had eaten part of his body to avoid starving to death themselves. John and his men took care of the first group. The second group then pushed on to Taos.

Kit Carson was a friend of John's for many years. Carson guided several expeditions. In the woodcut at left, Carson stands with his horse, Apache.

In His Own Words

Many people consider the fourth expedition a disaster. But John insisted it was a success. He wrote, "The result [of the expedition] was entirely satisfactory. It convinced me that neither snow of winter nor mountain ranges were obstacles in the way" of a transcontinental rail route.

One of John's men, Alexis Godey, was the hero of the expedition. He left Taos as soon as he could form a rescue party. In four days, he made it back to the mountains. He rescued 15 of John's men who might otherwise have died in the mountains. Ten other men died on the expedition.

John finally gave up surveying. Carson and his wife nursed John back to health. As soon as John was well, he left Taos for California. Along the way, he heard that gold had been discovered near Sutter's Fort in early 1848. He was excited because he had bought about 40,000 acres (16,200 hectares) of land near the gold fields. Later, gold was found on John's land, Las Mariposas. The Frémonts were rich.

In 1848, gold was discovered at Sutter's Mill. John became rich when gold was discovered on his land in the area. This photo was taken in the 1850s.

Chapter Five

Politics and Civil War

On September 9, 1850, California became a state. John was appointed one of California's first two U.S. senators. The Senate session in Washington, D.C., ended soon after California became a state. John's senatorial term ended after 21 days.

During the 1850s, slavery was legal in many states. John was against slavery, but many Californians disagreed with him. He was not reelected.

The Presidential Election of 1856

In 1855, members of the Democratic Party came to talk to John. This political party wanted John to run for president of the United States. They told John that as a Democrat, he had to support slavery. John hated slavery and refused to be the Democrats' candidate. Instead, the Democrats chose James Buchanan, who supported slavery.

The new Republican Party wanted a candidate who was against slavery.

This poster from the presidential election of 1856 shows
John (left) and his running mate, William Dayton.
That year, John ran for U.S. president as a Republican.

They asked John to run for president. He agreed. John's supporters walked through city streets chanting, "Free men, free speech, free soil, and Frémont!" Abraham Lincoln gave 90 speeches in support of John.

Millard Fillmore of the American Party was the third candidate for U.S. president. He already had been president from 1850 to 1853. The election of 1856 was close, and James Buchanan was elected president.

Army Career

In 1860, Abraham Lincoln was the Republican presidential candidate. He won the election. The slaveholding Southern states worried that Lincoln would outlaw slavery. Eleven states withdrew from the United States and started their own country, the Confederate States of America. This secession set the stage for the U.S. Civil War (1861–1865).

John offered to fight for the Northern states in the Civil War. President Lincoln asked him to command 30,000 soldiers in the border state of Missouri. Lincoln said the border states of Delaware,

Maryland, Kentucky, and Missouri could keep slaves if they remained loyal to the Northern states.

On August 30, 1861, John declared martial law in Missouri. This wartime action gave him the power to make political decisions in the state. He decided to free all the Missouri slaves. Lincoln was not yet ready to free any slaves. He worried that the action might cause the border states to join the South.

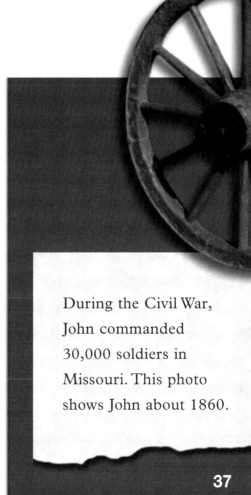

During the Civil War, John commanded 30,000 soldiers in Missouri. This photo shows John about 1860.

Lincoln told John to change his order. John refused, so Lincoln removed him from command. It was not until January 1863 that Lincoln issued the Emancipation Proclamation. This order finally freed the slaves, but only in Southern-held territory. The slaves in Missouri were not freed until after the war.

John's weary troops marched through Virginia during the Civil War. Confederate General Thomas Jackson defeated these troops five times in a row.

Emancipation Proclamation

At the start of the Civil War, President Lincoln's goal was to keep the United States together, not to free slaves. In 1863, he added the goal of freeing slaves. He issued the Emancipation Proclamation to free slaves in areas that the Southern armies held. The proclamation did not free slaves in the border states or in Southern areas under Union control. In December 1865, after the war's end, the 13th Amendment to the U.S. Constitution permanently outlawed slavery in the United States.

In March 1862, John was named commander of the army in western Virginia. John's soldiers were hungry and tired. They had to find their own food. John and his troops lost five battles in a row to Southern General Thomas "Stonewall" Jackson.

John's army life ended on August 12, 1863. President Lincoln decided to reorganize his small armies into one large army. When John heard that he was no longer in charge, he resigned.

Troubles

After the war, John had many troubles. He owned part of a western railroad, but it failed, and he lost most of his money. He fell deeply into debt and was forced to sell Las Mariposas to pay the money he owed. By the 1870s, John and Jessie lived off the money she earned as an author.

Shortly before his death in 1890, John's dark hair and beard had turned white.

With Jessie's help, John wrote *Memoirs of My Life*. This book told of John's life experiences. But people were no longer interested in John's life, and few people bought the book.

Death and Accomplishments

In July 1890, John visited New York State. During his visit, he became ill. A doctor determined that John's appendix had burst and infected his body. Early on the morning of July 13, 1890, John died at age 77. He was buried near Tarrytown, New York.

John was one of the last great western explorers. He journeyed through vast areas of land. His maps and descriptions of the Oregon Trail were clear and easy for others to follow. He told the truth about the areas he visited, even if it was a truth that not everyone always wanted to hear. His reports encouraged people to move west.

John did have his human faults. He sometimes did things without preparation. He did not always admit his mistakes. In spite of that, John truly earned his nickname of the "Pathfinder."

TIMELINE

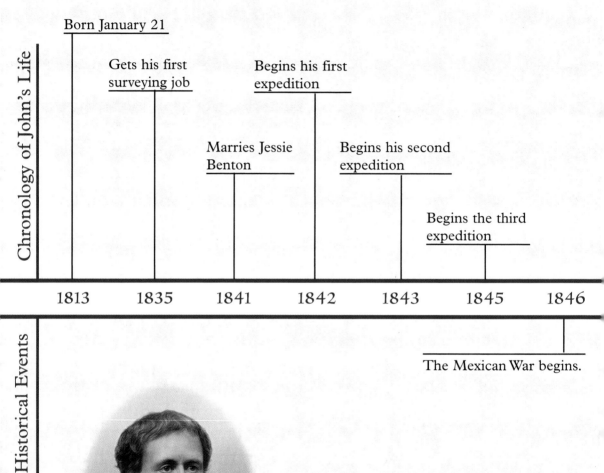

Chronology of John's Life

Born January 21

Gets his first surveying job

Begins his first expedition

Marries Jessie Benton

Begins his second expedition

Begins the third expedition

1813   1835   1841   1842   1843   1845   1846

Historical Events

The Mexican War begins.

After the Civil War ended, John sometimes wore his army uniform.

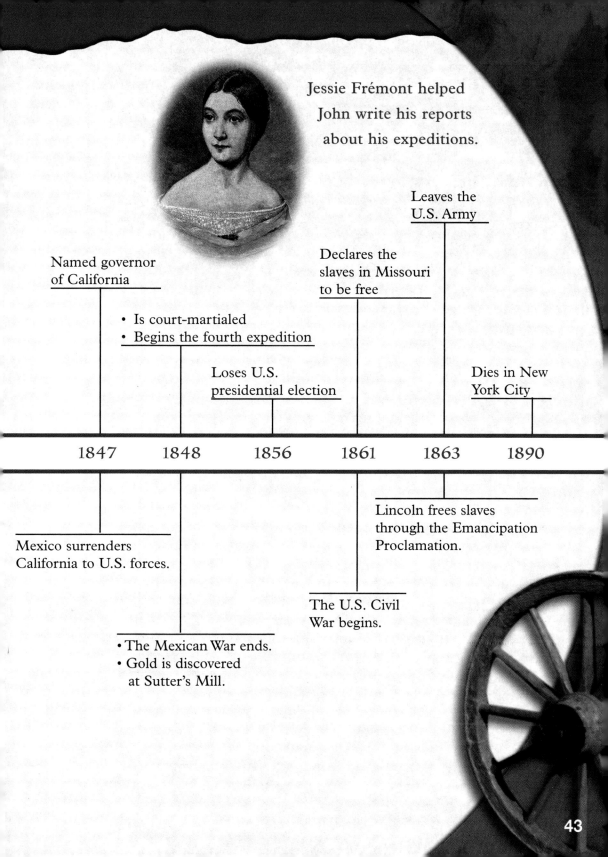

Jessie Frémont helped
John write his reports
about his expeditions.

Leaves the
U.S. Army

Named governor
of California

Declares the
slaves in Missouri
to be free

• Is court-martialed
• Begins the fourth expedition

Dies in New
York City

Loses U.S.
presidential election

1847	1848	1856	1861	1863	1890

Lincoln frees slaves
through the Emancipation
Proclamation.

Mexico surrenders
California to U.S. forces.

The U.S. Civil
War begins.

• The Mexican War ends.
• Gold is discovered
  at Sutter's Mill.

Glossary

astronomy (uh-STRON-uh-mee)—the study of stars, planets, and other objects in space

border state (BOR-dur STATE)—a state that allowed slavery during the U.S. Civil War but remained loyal to the Northern states; the border states were Kentucky, Delaware, Maryland, and Missouri.

court-martial (CORT-MAR-shuhl)—a military trial

expedition (ek-spuh-DISH-uhn)—a long trip of exploration

Los Osos (LOHSS OH-sohss)—a group of American settlers who fought against the Mexican government in California in 1846; Los Osos is a Spanish phrase that means "the bears."

Manifest Destiny (MAN-uh-fest DESS-tuh-nee)—the belief that God gave white Americans the right to take over lands that belonged to other people

martial law (MAR-shuhl LAW)—a wartime state of events that allows a military commander to make decisions for an area

opponent (uh-POH-nunht)—a person who is against another person

surrender (suh-REN-dur)—to give up or admit defeat in battle

survey (sir-VAY)—to measure land to make a map

For Further Reading

Jaffe, Elizabeth D. *The Oregon Trail.* Let Freedom Ring. Mankato, Minn.: Bridgestone Books, 2002.

Marcovitz, Hal. *John C. Frémont: Pathfinder of the West.* Explorers of New Worlds. Philadelphia: Chelsea House, 2002.

Monroe, Judy. *The California Gold Rush.* Let Freedom Ring. Mankato, Minn.: Bridgestone Books, 2002.

Stefoff, Rebecca. *First Frontier.* North American Historical Atlases. New York: Benchmark Books, 2000.

Places of Interest

Bent's Old Fort National Historic Site
35110 Highway 194 East
La Junta, CO 81050-9523
Visitors can view demonstrations of daily life in 1840s Colorado.

Campo de Cahuenga
3919 Lankershim Boulevard
North Hollywood, CA 91604
http://www.usc.edu/isd/archives/la/historic/campo_de_cahuenga.html
John and the Mexican leader signed an agreement here to end the Mexican War in California.

Frémont National Forest
Supervisor's Office
1301 South G Street
Lakeview, OR 97630
This national forest is named for John.

South Pass City Historic Site
125 South Pass Main
South Pass, WY 82520
http://spacr.state.wy.us/sphs/south.htm
The Oregon Trail passes this historic town near the South Pass Continental Divide.

Sutter's Fort
2701 L Street
Sacramento, CA 95816
The fort re-creates John Sutter's settlement in 1840s California.

Internet Sites

Captain John Charles Frémont and the Bear Flag Revolt
http://www.militarymuseum.org/fremont.html
John's activities in California are described at this site.

John Charles Frémont: Explorer, Mapmaker, Soldier
http://www.longcamp.com
Among much other information, this site describes John's route for his second expedition.

John Frémont 1813–1890
http://www.johnfremont.com
This site provides information about John's life; it contains many links to information about John.

Major General John C. Fremont: The Great Pathfinder
http://www.ironorchid.com/history/fremont/index.htm
A series of photographs illustrates different stages of John's life. Viewers can find many links to more information about John.

The Museum of Sutter's Fort
http://score.rims.k12.ca.us/activity/suttersfort
Visitors to this Internet site can enjoy a virtual tour of the museum at Sutter's Fort.

Index